ARCHITECTURE LANDSCAPE URBANISM 2

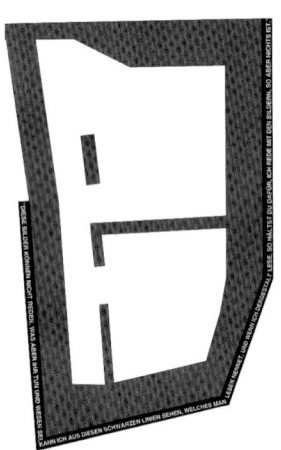

The drainage channel around the house is covered with steel plates, into which a quotation from HJC Grimmelshausen's *Der Abentheurliche Simplicissimus Teutsch* has been laser-cut:

'These figures cannot talk: but what they do and what they are, that can I see from these black lines, and that do men call reading. And when I thus do read, thou conceivest that I speak with the figures: but 'tis not so.'

Grimmelshausen was born in Gelnhausen in c. 1622. His *Simplicissimus* is the most important novel of the German Baroque.

LIVING ROOM

Architecture Landscape Urbanism 2: Living Room

Authors/Artists: M Christine Boyer, Peter Cook, Ludger Gerdes, David Heymann, Ottmar Hörl, Thomas Kling, Martha LaGess, Wolfgang Luy, Scott Murff, Gabriela Seifert, Catherine Spellman, Charly Steiger, Götz Stöckmann, Dalibor Vesely, Achim Wollscheid.

AA Publications are initiated by the Chairman of the Architectural Association, Mohsen Mostafavi.

The publication has been edited by Pamela Johnston and designed by Emily Bennett. Editorial Assistants: Clare Barrett, Mark Rappolt.

Translations from the German by Sunitha Amalraj, Petra Kayser and Catherine Schelbert.

Collaborators on the Living Room project: Nadine Aschenbrücker, Martin Böhler, Jan Peter Dahl, Barbara Eiden, Michael Fick, Martin Häusle, Friedrich Wilhelm Jakob, Joachim Keilbach, Markus Kilian, Ruth Knobloch, Anita Schmidt-Effing, Christian Schmutz, Roland Schnizer, Alexander Schranz, Nicole Weinbrecht.
Structural Engineer: Rüsch/Diem/Schuler of Dornbirn, Austria.

ISBN 1 870890 97 3

Contents © 1999
Architectural Association and the Artists and Authors
AA Publications
36 Bedford Square
London WC1B 3ES

No part of this book may be reproduced in any manner whatsoever without written permission from the publisher, except in the context of reviews.

Site plan showing location of project in Gelnhausen.

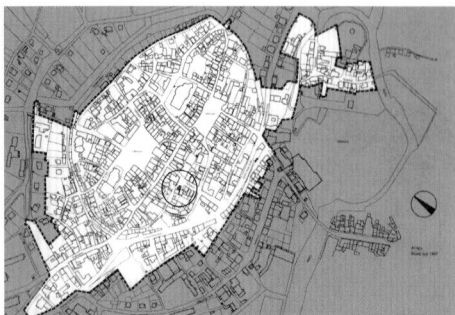

Writings
- **6 Gabriela Seifert and Götz Stöckmann** Parallel Horizons
- **8 M Christine Boyer** Playgrounds
- **10 Thomas Kling** The House is the Mouth Cave
- **12 Gabriela Seifert and Götz Stöckmann** The Transformation of No.15 Kuhgasse
- **22 Dalibor Vesely** The Poetics of Transformation
- **26 David Heymann** Correspondence, in Translation
- **32 Ludger Gerdes** Context?
- **35 Martha LaGess** Covered by Sky, Open to Ground
- **45 Achim Wollscheid** Context! (An Alternative View)
- **50 Peter Cook** A Heart's Project
- **54 Biographical Notes**

Lyrics
- **2 Memorial to HJC Grimmelshausen**
- **56 Thomas Kling** Epigram for the Lemon House

Mappings
- **23 Catherine Spellman and Scott Murff** Here and Gone

Artworks
- **30 Ottmar Hörl** Photography: Making Contact
- **38 Ludger Gerdes** Painting
- **40 Charly Steiger** Light: Flicker
- **42 Achim Wollscheid** Noise: Transformation
- **48 Wolfgang Luy** Sculpture

Architecture/Landscape
- **12 Gabriela Seifert and Götz Stöckmann** Building Description

Appendix
- **52 Thomas Kling** Das Haus ist der Mundraum

Parallel Horizons
Gabriela Seifert and Götz Stöckmann

Adam's house in paradise, Laugier's primitive hut, Viollet-le-Duc's dome of tree branches, all are based upon the premise that architecture came into being as a representation or interpretation of nature. They recognize nature as the basis for architectural form, from the universal gabled house to the sophisticated column order. We, however, try to see nature, not as a formal model, but as the horizon onto which we position our building.

> Cicero explains:
> …columns support the structure of the temple and the hall, and yet this function in no way exceeds their beauty. The pediment…, and the temple as a whole, were surely not determined by beauty but by considerations of usefulness. However, in fulfilling its function, allowing the rain to drain away on both sides, the pediment's usefulness is enhanced by its dignity; and if the temple stood in the heavens, without the pediment, it would not possess the dignity that so befits it…

The new house at no. 15 Kuhgasse is intended to be a fundamental building, the minimum needed to create a living room, a protective shell. The structure will be concealed within the three-dimensional interior surfaces. The appearance of the shell will be reduced to a geometry of mass and openings – a membrane separating the exterior from the interior.

We have commissioned artists working in a variety of mediums to devise the decoration of the house. We hope that the combination of their art and their poetry with our architecture will increase the house's pictorial and linguistic power, forming a new context with which to address the public.

Indeed, the house and this publication share this aspect in common. All of the artworks and texts were developed in parallel, without reference to each other; but all of them unite the place and the house.

We will install a stony landscape in the house. We dream about this small place reaching the horizon, where the sky may fall on our heads…

View of Gelnhausen, with
Church of Our Lady in the foreground.

LIVING ROOM

Playgrounds
M Christine Boyer

Once upon a time, there was a crooked wooden house of a funny yellow colour that stood at the corner of some meandering lanes in an old medieval town. It was a simple house, never pretending to be noble. For three hundred years it formed just one element of an inconspicuous backdrop to events great and small. Yet the humble house had charm and told a multitude of tales. Viewed from the street, it resembled a child's drawing with a door and six windows on its facade and smoke unfurling from its stack. It suggested an image of blissful innocence. The old medieval town became the playground for two high-school students who, ignorant of the passage of time and blind to the weight of history, passed by the simple house on the way to their favourite haunts. When they returned to the town as architecture students, the wistful house was still waiting. As witness to the upside-down nature of the world, it bridged the gap between the marginal realm of childhood play and the adult order of seriousness and control, to become their new playground.

Children like to play games: they mark off the territory for their playground and establish their own set of rules. And so these architects, in their free time, began to manipulate the rules of their game. The house is classified as part of the historic fabric of the town, and should be protected by severe codes of preservation; but it is literally coming apart at the seams, so the architects have been given permission to demolish it and build a new house in its place. Just the outline of the old yellow house is to be retained while the interior is opened up to play, infiltrated with ideas, and deepened with time.

If the old house is to be razed and its image eradicated from memory, then its demolition has to be treated with respect. In a spirit of satirical play there will be a proper farewell ceremony, when hundreds of red carnations will be arranged in a decorative grid across the house's facade and sides. What causes spontaneous laughter when this image of the house with its carnations is projected on the screen is, perhaps, the unexpected shifting of the sanctimonious rules and rituals of patrimony. Now it is the field of patrimony that becomes paradoxical and problematic while the manoeuvres of the guileless play triumphant. The overdetermined historic certainty of the house's place in the town is upset by a playful sequence of moves that shifts the conventional game towards the uncertain, the incomplete, the unknown. The rude red carnations and the rational grid, the impromptu and the regulated, mock the rituals they imitate and invest them with festive seriousness.

When the balloon structure of the new house arises it will be clad in chipboard and asphalt paper and will receive a new blessing. But the house is in no hurry to be finished – it beckons one to come inside, be still, go slow. Eventually it may be clad in smooth seamless sheets of aluminium, and after that perhaps paved in stone. But meanwhile it has been set aside as a playground for the architects, five artists and a poet. The walls will become more open than closed when fifty-two windows of vernacular size and shape puncture the volume. Windows are a frame on reality, an interface between inside and out, but here their exaggerated number and serial arrangement will set up a tension between the real and the fictive, between the children outside and the grown-ups within.

In the depths of the house will be located a cabinet of photographs: a vertical catalogue of views looking out through the windows. The one at the top of the pile may be no more important than the one at the bottom, for the arrangement is entirely arbitrary. The photographs form an inventory: they assess, add up and store – in what promises to be an infinite and humorous array – the irreversible flow of views from inside to out. What is it like to experience the interior of the house as inhabited, to feel the paradox that marks the gathering inwards of stillness and the flowing outwards of energy towards the town?

This new house is alive: it speaks, it lights up, it opens out, it tastes and smells. It writes its messages on its walls, turning speech into a spatial act to be read on the horizontal surfaces of its exterior. This writing house – or mouth cave – comments on and reframes the acts of remembrance and replacement, looking cautiously at renewal and play. Defying common-sense procedures, it displays an epigram written for all the generations who have inhabited the old house, and all those who will inhabit the new one, which voices fears about what the neighbours might say about the house's upside-down, inside-out playfulness.

If the hearth of the house is to be found at the top, on a cantilever box that projects outwards towards the city, then the ground floor contains a rock garden. Once again inversions are set into play. Tradition tells us to expect a house with doors and windows and a series of rooms, not a house of many windows and only one room. Common sense reminds us that a garden grows on the outside, as it needs sun, rain and light; it is not an interior landscape of boulders. But then the order of a game is not a natural order: it transgresses common sense. This new playground challenges any idea that tradition is stable or offers coherence over time, for things are suspended, undecided, deferred. The new house imperfectly maps itself onto the parameters of the conventional world. Its order is emergent, open-ended and incomplete as it playfully adds things up, proliferates and crosses thresholds in defiance of stable meanings and order.

The House is the Mouth Cave
Thomas Kling

the house is the mouth cave.
the house is the text of its inhabitants.

is it fair to speak of the breath,
the deep breath of the people living in the house?

is it fair to speak of the breath
of generations that have lived in the house?

bad breath in a stuffy house. odours in the stairwell
and from the windows in the neighbourhood

breath from the woman who just gave birth
fast breath, rattling, of someone dying.

the windows are open, the front door opens,
a person leaves the house, hesitates, turns around,

goes back into the house, returns with an object
forgotten the first time, it is 10:35.

is it fair to speak of the breath of the inhabitants
and their forgetfulness ? of the speed with which

a deserted house becomes a deserted house?
is it fair to say that the stones inside the house

come unexpectedly? is it fair to say that big stones
have ended up in the middle of the living room

where they don't belong? what, son, will the neighbours say?
son, have you thought about what the neighbours

will say? the neighbours breathe in their houses,
mother, they leave the house, turn back because they

have forgotten something, but, son, what will your neighbours
say when they discover that the garden is in the house?

mother, my garden breathes in the house, breathes like
my neighbours do. everybody has plants in their house, mother!

i turn around, i turn the house around because i forgot
something. i have turned the house upside down!

is it fair, son, to talk about the house breathing
so hard that the second floor can drive on the street!

mother, all the neighbours will want a ride when they see
what my house can do. the house yawns, it breathes, mother!

the house tastes its inhabitants, it opens its mouth cave.
the house breathes, it is the text of its inhabitants.

the house is at home with itself, it shows itself, it shows
the sum of its breath: the house is the mouth cave.

Translation by Catherine Schelbert.

The Transformation of No. 15 Kuhgasse

Gabriela Seifert and Götz Stöckmann

Houses appear to have an everyday presence: a continual existence. Houses grow old with the passing of the seasons. Houses store history, the life of a town: growth, prosperity, advancement, fall, flames, storms, war. Destruction and reconstruction, innovation. Continually.

The house at no. 15 Kuhgasse, Gelnhausen, was probably built soon after the end of the Thirty Years War, using material reclaimed from the ruins of the town. It was never a fine building: neither dignified in appearance, nor possessing artisanal charm. Its walls had no proportional order, no ornament of any kind, but were rendered yellow, giving rise to its local nickname: '*Zitronehäus'che*' (Lemon House). Yet the house somehow insinuated itself into our possession. It was a lively, bright place, cosy in the winter, cheerful and alive in the warm days of the summer. In short, it had a fine location in the town, which we wanted to make something good out of.

Gelnhausen was founded in the twelfth century, and quickly achieved city status. Its medieval landmarks include the Staufer palace, by Friedrich Barbarossa, and the famous rood loft in the Romanesque/Gothic Church of Our Lady. Gelnhausen was also the birthplace of Grimmelshausen, who wrote the first German-language novel, *Der Abentheurliche Simplicissimus Teutsch*.

The whole of the old town is a conservation area. Four houses down the road, at no. 5 Kuhgasse, is a splendid half-timber house, the oldest in Hesse. We asked ourselves what we could do with our crumbling house. We had discussions with the town council, with the conservation department and with structural engineers, but found nothing that would warrant its restoration. Finally, we made the decision to demolish it and build something new.

We designed a house for the small site which – in accordance with conservation regulations – replicated the volume and geometry of the old building. Everything else we did differently.

We wanted the small house to have a sense of largeness, so we made a single big room that extends from the floor to the gable, from one external wall to the other. We wanted openness – from outside to inside, and vice versa – so we covered the walls and roof with an extensive, rigorous grid of windows, and added battlements to the gable. We sought to establish connections with the ground, the earth, the horizon, so we designed the interior as a stony landscape, with gravel, rocks, large boulders and a sparse planting of evergreens.

All service spaces, such as the kitchen, WC, bath, heating, ventilation and archive, are small and incorporated into a hollow gable wall. A box suspended between the gable walls contains the private spaces: a sleeping cell with a deck and hearth on top. The high deck offers views over the rooftops of the town, out across the Spessart landscape.

We wanted the house to have an independent form within the context of the historic town. Not alien, nor familiar; not off-putting, but tactful. We have respected the geometry and small scale of the locale, but have made the typology cleaner. We have given order to the elevations and covered everything with a unifying material: roof and wall, outside and inside – all have the same smooth skin. The house,

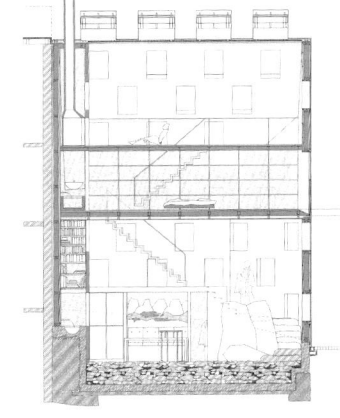

almost model-like, hides the details of its construction: it has no roof tiles, no gutters, no window handles. We have attempted to design a structure with the same rhythm on roof and wall; with closed surfaces for art installations, pictures and ornament; with open surfaces for light and views. No tectonics, no legible storeys, but an overplayed entrance. A building as a membrane between interior and exterior.

During the planning phase we invited artists to develop works for the house. These span a wide range of mediums: there is poetry, painting, sculpture, photography, sound-art (noise), and an installation with strobe lights. We consciously chose artists who have different concepts of the function of art in society. Some believe in the autonomy of art, while others attempt, with their work, to intervene in everyday life and social processes.

This book contains two commentaries by artists whose work exemplifies these different approaches. Ludger Gerdes's facade paintings represent architectural and landscape themes. They are self-contained pictures. Reproduced on the house's walls, they articulate the relations between the building and its surroundings. But they could equally, as framed pictures, occupy a completely different location. The art of Achim Wollscheid, on the other hand, deals with the sounds in the street outside. Environmental noise is recorded and transformed via programmed composition-presets, then emitted in real time in the interior of the house. The artwork

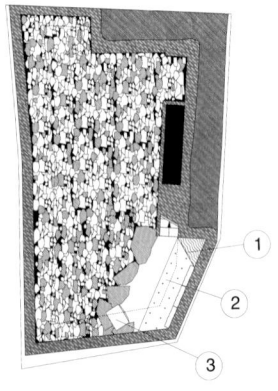
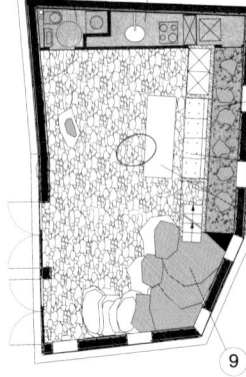
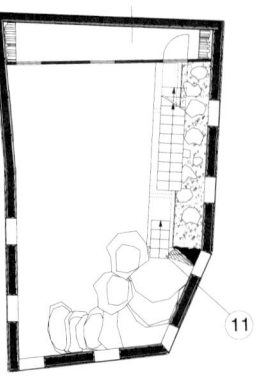

Basement - 0.80   Ground floor + 0.00   Mezzanine + 2.50

Key
1 Pond
2 Chaise longue
3 Monitor

4 WC
5 Pantry
6 Flower bed/stepping stones
7 Loggia/bench
8 Luy's table
9 Boulders/heap

10 Archive
11 Well

12 Bathroom
13 Sleeping
14 Projecting room

15 Open fire
16 Deck

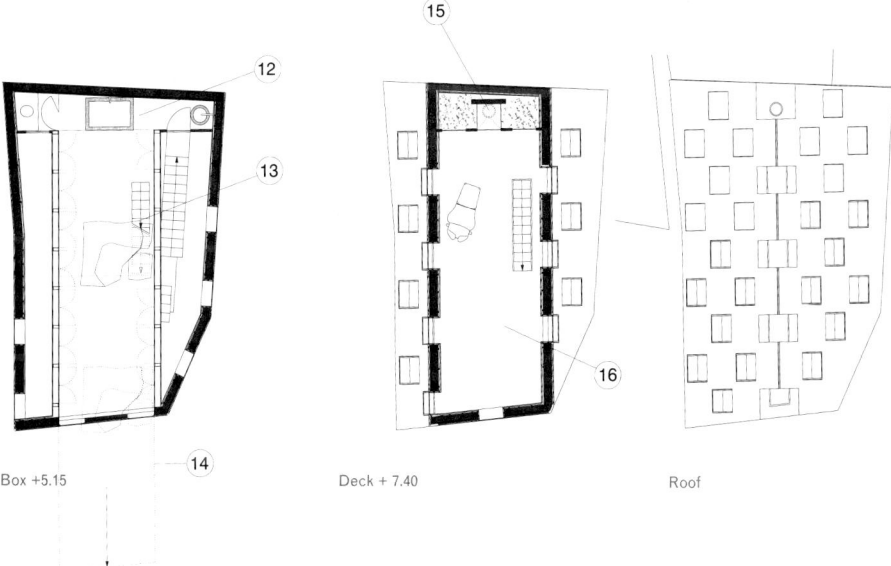

Box +5.15   Deck + 7.40   Roof

LIVING ROOM

is specifically tied to the place. Two different works – two different mindsets. We hope that these differences will intensify the dialogue between the house and its surroundings.

In the beginning we attempted to assign specific places in and around the house to individual artists, but soon abandoned this idea, as it proved incompatible with our desire to allow a completely independent approach to the given theme: the house and the locale. Here a dilemma arose: who should do what, and in what order? Should we, as the architects and initiators of the project, remain purely the clients for the artworks? Or could we strive for an interplay between art and architecture that might give the house a stronger voice?

We will see. In classical times a close collaboration between disciplines could produce a total artwork, combining building, painting and sculpture. Such works would be defined by artistic conventions and codes, and have a noble or sacred purpose. But what is the over-riding purpose of the Kuhgasse house; where is the common ground?

The discipline, content and chosen medium of the artworks in the Kuhgasse house derive from the artist's own sensibilities. This is a collection of individual positions. The artworks created here have no over-riding content. They have only the place and the house in common – the parallel circumstances of their conception.

Perhaps this combination of landscape, lyrics, painting, sculpture, architecture, prose, traces of the old house, sound and light will create a work with its own context. An 'open' station for different artistic, architectural and poetic positions.

Everything is orientated 'inwards' as well as 'outwards'.
But not in a representative way.
The house stands for itself and awaits a response.

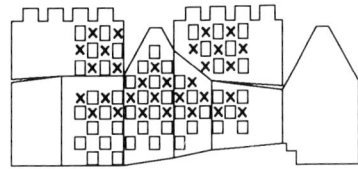

Ludger Gerdes: Painting
Large paintings on exterior walls and roof.

Charly Steiger: Light
Spellman/Murff mappings/models.
Strobe light illuminating models in boxes, which are visible through viewing slits in the facade.

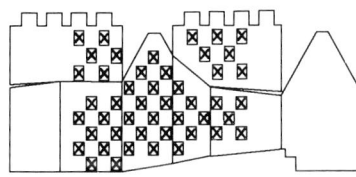

Ottmar Hörl: Photography
Photographs of all views from all windows, looking outwards, installed in an archive.

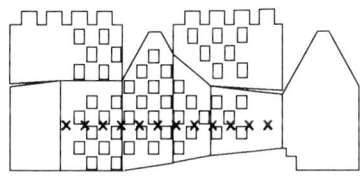

Thomas Kling: Poetry
Epigram on the temporary asphalt sheeting facade.
Poems on the front gate.

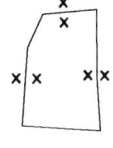

Achim Wollscheid: Noise
Electronic transfer of external sound into the interior space (and vice-versa); three-dimensional sound composition.

Wolfgang Luy: Sculpture
Table installation in the landscape.

Bye-bye Kuhgasse 15. Installation with 2,500 red carnations.

Boulder landscape assembly.

Topping-out ceremony with ICHS installation by Ludger Gerdes.

18 SIX STAGES OF TRANSFORMATION

Asphalt sheeting with epigram by Thomas Kling.

White sprayed aluminium sheeting, a canvas for paintings by Ludger Gerdes.

Stone coating and dormer windows to conform with conservation regulations.

LIVING ROOM

LIVING ROOM interior. Left: looking down the stairwell. Right: ground floor.

The Poetics of Transformation
Dalibor Vesely

The nature of modern architecture has in recent years reached a point where the pluralism of individual positions threatens to become a dogmatically frozen reality. The dogmatism and apparent fatality of the situation, however, obscure the real nature of the problem. They obscure the fact that pluralism is not produced by the confrontation of different positions, but is a result of a long process of rationalization of culture which has eroded the common ground of understanding and sharing and reduced individual positions to fragments of introverted culture.

The same process has separated the anonymous rationalized public domain of architecture from the relative richness of its private domain. Because architecture is a discipline rooted in culture, its success or failure always depends on a certain unity of meaning. Such unity will be established wherever it is historically and culturally possible. In our current culture, it is in the private dwelling that unity of meaning is expected to be attainable. This should not surprise us. The private dwelling has for some time been seen as an important repository of meaning, and its role could very well be compared with the role played in the past by the city and by public buildings and spaces.

The modern house is not a phenomenon *sui generis* but only a particular historical form of dwelling. Its origins coincide with the crisis of the city in the Renaissance, when the first successful attempts were made to move away from the difficulties of urban life in order to create a more perfect way of life, first in the country and later in the city itself. Private galleries of paintings and sculpture, libraries, salons for political and private debates, rooms for music and entertainment: these are some of the items, or rather fragments, of introverted culture which illustrate the transformation of traditional public life into its private modern equivalent. This change is best sumarized by the well-known phrase: a city is a large house and a house is a small city.

The private house was, and in a way still is, the key reference in the formation of the modern city and of modern culture. In the general tendency to create an ideal setting for private life, it was not only the private house that came into existence but also the private garden. The garden became the domain where the domestic representation of culture could be completed on a cosmic level. It was the means to fulfil the vision of a terrestrial paradise, the vision of innocence and private salvation which has motivated the history of the private house from the very beginning. This vision inevitably refers to a more primordial mode of being and thus to memory, which makes the house a unique place of recollection and a unity of culture as a whole.

The fact that the private house became a repository for the most introverted culture, and, at the same time, a potential vehicle for an authentic cultural recollection and renewal, is the most interesting aspect of its history. This intriguing duality may explain why it is that the private house and the museum have become such prominent themes in recent architectural development. The same duality may also help us to see why a deep understanding of the nature of the modern house may lead to a more authentic vision of architecture in the future.

Among the more recent attempts to demonstrate such a possibility belongs the house at no. 15 Kuhgasse in Gelnhausen. The attempt to address in a new way the question of the private and the public is based on the principles of negation, inversion and sublimation. The neutral, repetitive and anonymous treatment of the outside is also applied inside the building, negating the traditional distinction between the public and the private. This opens up a possibility for the more radical step of bringing the outside literally inside, in the form of a garden. The introduction of the garden into the house extends the process of negation towards full inversion. The open space of the garden becomes a room, the trees and vegetation become stones and solid ground, the setting to see and experience becomes a setting to live in. Together with the open volume, the garden introduces the vertical arrangement and reading of the house. The arrangement itself is not only conceptual but also dreamlike. It appears that a gentle but firm force draws dreams always towards the height. Dreams of height give sustenance to our instinct of verticality. In communing through imagination with the verticality of upright objects and their arrangement, we experience the beneficial influence of lifting forces, we participate in the forms assured of their verticality. The ascending movement from the garden through the rest of the house is pre-eminently a symbol of the passage from one mode of living to another. The sequence of levels, focused on the only enclosed room of the house, the exemplary space of dreams, culminates in the transparent roof communicating with the sky. The sublimation of the ground into a dream-like nature of continuous walls, roof and sky is in many ways a recollection of the origins of the new house – the demolition of the old house and its reincarnation in the new one.

The ruins of the old house appear suddenly full of significance, in that they express the collapse of the old times; the ghost that haunts them indicates a peculiarly intense fear of the return of the powers of the past. In this way the old house becomes a sublimated vision similar to the vision of an ideal work of art described by André Breton in 'L'Amour Fou':

> The work of art, just like any fragment of human life considered in its deepest meaning, seems to be devoid of value if it does not offer the hardness, the rigidity, the regularity, the lustre of the crystal on every interior and exterior facet....
>
> The house where I live, my life, what I write: I dream that all these things might appear from far off like these cubes of rock salt close up.

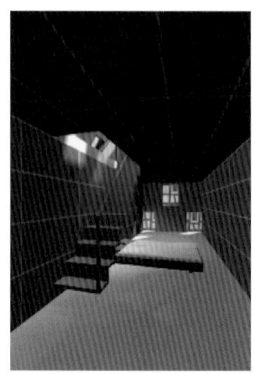

LIVING ROOM interior.
Left: on the deck. Right: inside the box.

Here and Gone

Catherine Spellman and Scott Murff

The idea for this drawing project originated in the request from Seifert and Stöckmann to document the house before it is torn down. Today the house is in a state of abandon and uncertainty. Tenuously connected to its past history, it is now understood in terms of its eventual removal and replacement. Its past and future architectures are fundamentally tied to one another. The form of the past house defines that of the future house, the programme of the future responds to that of the past; and the surrounding situation remains the same. As such, the existing house occupies an ambiguous territory between the past and the future, at once here and gone.

Not being involved in the conception of the Gelnhausen project, our relationship to the house is analogous to its ambiguous state. We have no fixed images of the house as an object and no preconceptions about its future relationship to the town.

We began by asking several students to photograph the house in response to a series of topics. These photographs offer a view at once connected to the house, to its present situation, and to an occupant. Our perceptions of the house were formulated through the investigative process of piecing together fragmentary views from the photographs.

With these views, we began a reconstruction of the house. This led to three interpretations, each providing a momentary and fragmentary understanding of the place. These 'houses' were drawn, built in model, and then compared with the plans and sections. The discrepancies between our impressions and the actual building allude to the synthetic and participatory nature of architecture. The comparisons reveal a reality different from that presented by the plans or by our drawings of the house. The drawings speak of architecture defined by constant change, multiple readings and varied experience. In the second investigation, the overall space is dematerialized in favour of the detail. Each drawing presents a piece of the existing building at full scale, caught within the confines of the individual drawing frame.

The results of this study offer a series of views of the existing house rather than a singular reductive definition of it acknowledging the space between appearance and reality. The material illustrated here attempts to erase any absolute system of knowledge, producing instead multiple readings of the house and an occupant's relationship to it. We think of this material not so much as representations of the existing building, but as re-creations of it. The whole is described through the consideration of its parts. The drawing project seeks to capture our perceptions and the uncertain present in which the house exists.

  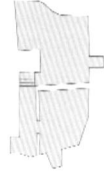 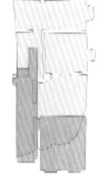 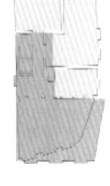  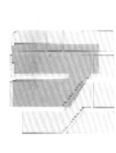

plan cellar   plan 1st floor   plan 2nd floor   plan attic   section

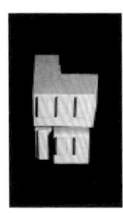     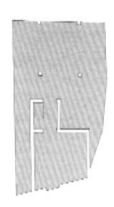 

discrepancy cellar   discrepancy 1st floor   discrepancy 2nd floor   discrepancy attic   section

 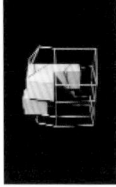 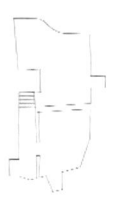   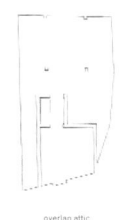 

overlap cellar   overlap 1st floor   overlap 2nd floor   overlap attic   section

SPELLMAN AND MURFF

We would like to acknowledge the assistance of Arizona State University students in the making of this project.

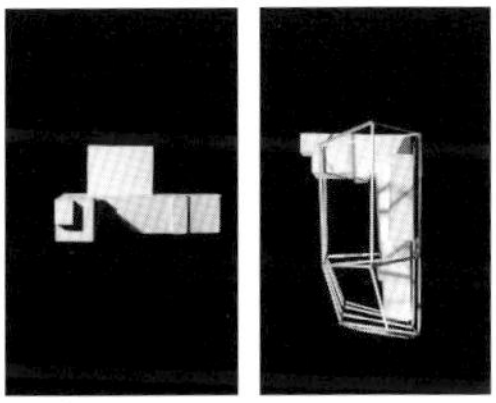

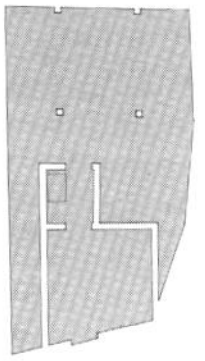

plan cellar	plan 1st floor	plan 2nd floor	plan attic	section
discrepancy cellar	discrepancy 1st floor	discrepancy 2nd floor	discrepancy attic	section
overlap cellar	overlap 1st floor	overlap 2nd floor	overlap attic	section

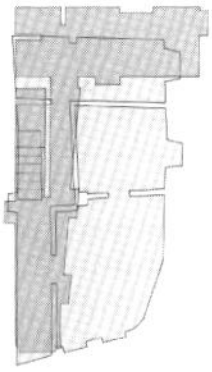

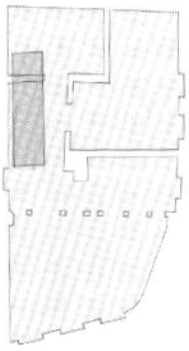

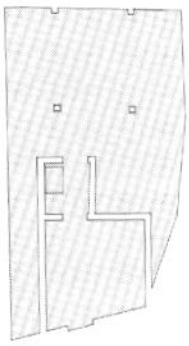

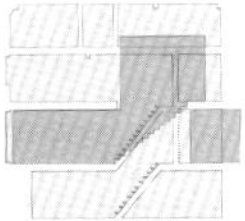

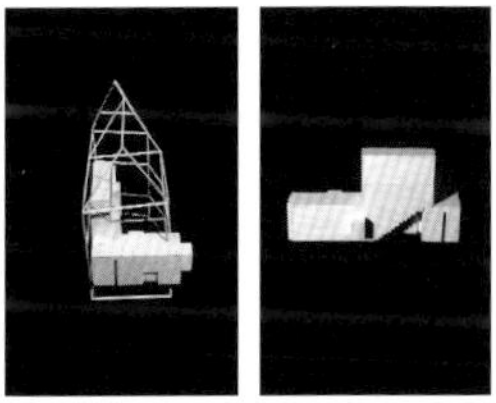

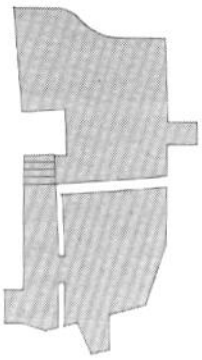

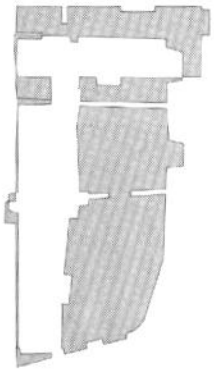

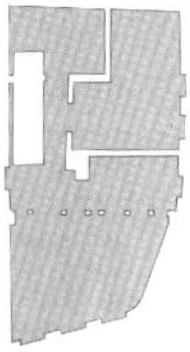

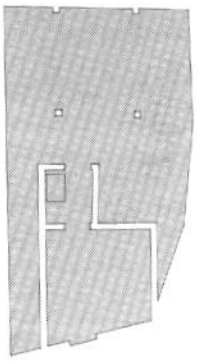

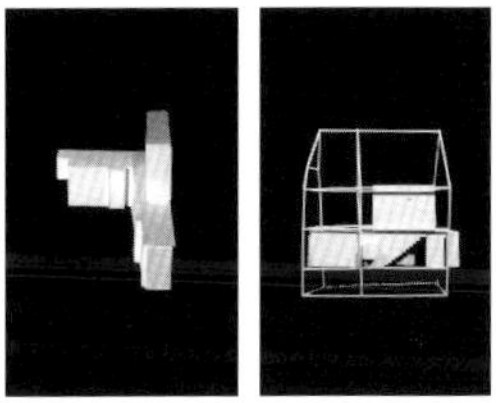

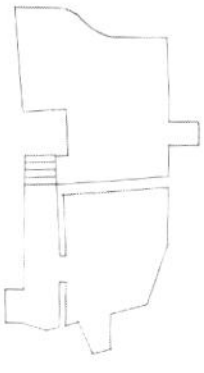

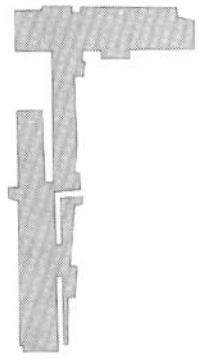

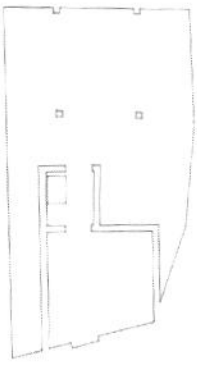

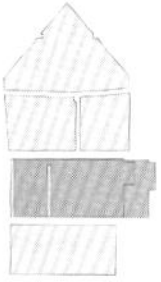

LIVING ROOM 25

Correspondence, in Translation
David Heymann, editor

In early June the *Frankfurter Allgemeine Zeitung* [*FAZ*] published a short article describing Seifert and Stöckmann's project for a house in the relatively intact medieval centre of Gelnhausen. The article, 'Notschrei, Notlandung, Notwendigkeit, oder Notwehr in Altstadt Gelnhausen?', by the journalist Thomas Villhauer, briefly speculated on the architects' intentions, as made evident through the publication of design documents, and the onset of construction.

To the extent that the *Zeitung* serves a large readership, Villhauer sought broad representative opinions both for and against the design. Included in the article is thus a rather pointed statement from a neighbour, identified here only as N (names are obscured at *FAZ* counsel's request): '...what tired purpose [*abgestanden Zweck*] does it serve for these two to set their needs over and against the desires of so many? Surely we have matured past such tomfoolery....'

The newspaper received just over four hundred letters in response to this quote, and published a selection of them on its editorial page. Shortly thereafter, it received a letter from the same N quoted in the initial article, in specific reply to comments, printed below, contained in a letter from a writer identified here as A. This second letter from N elicited further replies, and for several weeks N kept up a running dialogue with a series of correspondents, through the forum of the *Zeitung*. This correspondence is summarized here in chronological excerpts, translated into English.

The Villhauer article appeared on June 4. The first wave of letters arrived on June 5 and 6. This letter, from A, was published on June 7:

...although it is not explicitly stated, N seems to imply that we could rather easily build the city to appear as it has always done, and that we should do so. This recurring fantasy would seem to spring from a larger desire to have a landscape that we can say is stable, or perhaps better: secure [*sicher*]. But what sort of security is gained by such means? In New York City I can purchase a fraudulent Rolex watch for next to nothing, and in wearing it fool most. Unfortunately, whatever stability I have gained in my appearance, I have borrowed against my conscience. We can refill each empty lot with the most perfect replicants, yet behind the facade of such a city sit the inhabitants, nervously hoping the tourists will not notice, and waiting out those who remember. Under their feet the ground is like pudding.

Favouring general desire over personal certainty in such instances may seem the least offensive alternative, but in truth it serves no one well, nor even tolerably, and cannot be characterized as mature. In setting out to make our world secure, we conjure a virtual city of personal instability. The house in question would seem to point this out rather diagnostically, with its single chamber set alone in a landscape brought inside. If perhaps its inhabitants live their lives set out for others to see, in so doing they renegotiate a social contract that is not based on appearances.

As noted above, the *FAZ* then received this reply from N, which was published, excerpted as below, on June 11.
A speaks of the building as diagnosis, yet since when is it the role of a building to act as a diagnosis of anything, much less of the state of society? If I go to the doctor, and he tells me I have cancer, then am I cured? To the extent that architects have sought the role enjoyed by artists, to criticize, so have they abandoned the traditional ability of buildings to act as a cure of sorts, an antidote, to the world as they see it. It is one thing to say: *this is Germany, ill*. It is another to say so in stone, or, in this case, aluminium chequerboard. In Germany over these last thirty years much has been made of the individual's right to the public expression of his or her private apprehension of the world. Yet over that same time we have made little progress when it comes to answering the question: why should any one person's autobiography be considered culture?

On June 12, a Saturday, the *FAZ* again received a wave of letters in response to N. This letter, from a writer here called B, was printed on Monday, June 14:
…why does N invoke culture as a means to stifle culture? This is a frightening pathological behaviour, that seeks to restrain the future with the heavy muzzle of the past. There are perpetually two components to culture, one active, one passive. The passive component dwells within things, such as artworks, buildings, or landscapes, when these are seen to stand as answers to larger cultural questions. So we can speak of an evolving apprehension of the world based solely on the difference between a Romanesque and a Gothic arch! The active component of culture resides in the questions that prompt all such answers, and in the difficulty and inherent worth of such questions. So, for example, we could ask: should we allow this house? Or we could ask a more difficult question: given the terms of the house itself, is it a good design, or merely good because it is not like its surroundings?
It is a rule in the making of culture that the same artefact never suffices to answer the same question asked twice over time. The dialogue of culture is subtly amended by each answer, each artwork, given. Hence we do not accept as art something 'painted

in the style of'. The artwork is not merely the object: recognize, too, the struggle inherent in its inception.

So in the house it is possible to ascertain certain over-arching questions: What is inside and what is out? What is private, and what is not? What is nature, and where should one dwell in regard to it? What are the roles of circumstance and control? Who is the author? Who has authority? etc., etc... A new building 'made in the style of' cannot resurrect its putative origin. It is by default bound to a question: Why can we not make an art of today? Those who wish the past upon the future can be certain that such an attitude will guarantee further challenges!

On June 15, a third letter from N arrived at the *FAZ* offices (published June 16):
B's lecture in a letter notwithstanding, the world may indeed change, but there is no law or purpose that says it has to appear to change. Furthermore the notion that the method of the world, its age and its means, must be evident in its artefacts, is a relatively recent, a Modern, notion. It is an option [*Wahl*] only, a possibility, but it is not a probability, as is, say ... gravity!

It remains that the work of the architect, seen beyond the narrow confines of the profession and the exigencies of practicality, makes landscape, of a sort perhaps less interpretable than that made by the artist, perhaps more so than that made by the engineer. This categorical phenomenon of perception, that buildings cannot be thought about very much, remains insurmountable. So it is helpful to think of the architect's performance as the labour, rather than the building. Much value is bound up in interpretation, as in the interpretation of the same score, again and again, over the years. I stand against this house much as I would stand against the sour note played by the bassoonist who squeaks in revolt in the middle of the finale. It is that which stays in mind as you leave the Opera, rendering null and void the work of all others, souring the evening. Now I will live in the neighbourhood of the White House, or the Encephalitic Ice Cube, or the Euclidean Swiss Cheese, or the House of the Exhibitionist, or, worst of all, the *Haus der Architekten*, which is redundant, an abomination.

This letter – the writer is identified only as C – was published June 20:
N chooses to see a piece of property only as the last gasp of the cultural process of settlement, by which the world strains to subdivide itself into ever smaller units. What a story that is: wars, titles, grants; the arrival of common law and the property in abstract, endless debate and disagreement, jurisprudence; possessing, and the succession of conflicting claims, measuring, and measuring again. When the property is finally delivered, still steaming, to the landowner, it would seem only reason-

able that he or she should have the decency to respect the enormity of the effort! But any piece of property can also be the first step in the making of a new world, the first cell that mutates to a more correct constitution of domestic life. All such evolutionary experiments are ventures justified after the fact. We are overly concerned with our inability to dream certain dreams, yet give little credence to the tools necessary to do so. Sleep over the street? I prefer that to Disney World-Oompahland.

On June 24 the *FAZ* printed this excerpt from N's reply:
Only a two-dimensional moralist like C would insist that humans cannot see beyond the veil of appearances, and should therefore never be so fooled. So we hear once again that Disney World is evil. But no one is asking for Disney; I too am opposed in principle. The house in question, if I understand its theme of nature and voyeur, is as committed as a television to the artificial. The dichotomy of real and not real is a tiring hoax perpetrated by closet-materialists under the banner: We Know Better!

Finally, on June 27, the *FAZ* printed this curious letter from a writer D. It was the last letter printed on the subject, as by then public attention was fully focused on the scandals surrounding the Finance Minister.
Both C and N express justifiable concerns. I would only add that Disney World has several desirable qualities as a city model. First, it is entirely accessible to the disabled, a true wheelchair democracy. Second, children can there experience crowds without fear. Third, certain restaurants are carefully developed in such a manner that waiters distract children, or supervise them in overseeable yet discrete activity zones (one sand-bottomed play pool is immediately adjacent to a hot-tub, the far end of which – too deep for the children – is a sunken margarita bar).
The American State of Florida, in which Disney World is located, has, of course, an understandable grim notoriety among German visitors, and people there seem consequently more sensitive to our concerns. Still, a young tour guide at the Busch Gardens [a tourist attraction], apparently a college graduate, told [my husband and I] that she believed that we Germans were not allowed to take down the Berlin Wall until we had perfected the home cappuccino-maker! This opinion, slyly given, stayed with me initially because of its lunacy; only gradually did it begin to make sense. The crisis of domesticity is always, actually, political. The extent to which the outer wall of any house acts as the frontier [*Grenze*] between explicit ideologies of publicity and privacy marks it forever as a no man's land. I don't care what those architects do: I am not willing to wage another war over yet another boundary in our midst.

Photography: Making Contact
Ottmar Hörl

Seifert and Stöckmann's design for the Kuhgasse house pivots around the unconventional structure of the window openings. By means of this constant structure, the house conveys a formal totality which offers a visual demonstration – and methodical definition – of the reciprocity of interior and exterior. On the one hand the structure of the windows opens up the building, on the other hand this perforation creates an active, sensuous presence.

The presence of light and of views, the spatial tension between inside and outside, determine my engagement with the building – a documentation of the entire sequence of window openings as a recording of moments.

The camera captures the view through each opening from the inside looking out, each time from the same position – the eye level of a person of average height. The black-and-white photographic material will be enlarged to 24 x 30 cm and framed. Installed in a specially designed shelving system, the pictures of 'Making Contact' will form an archival record.

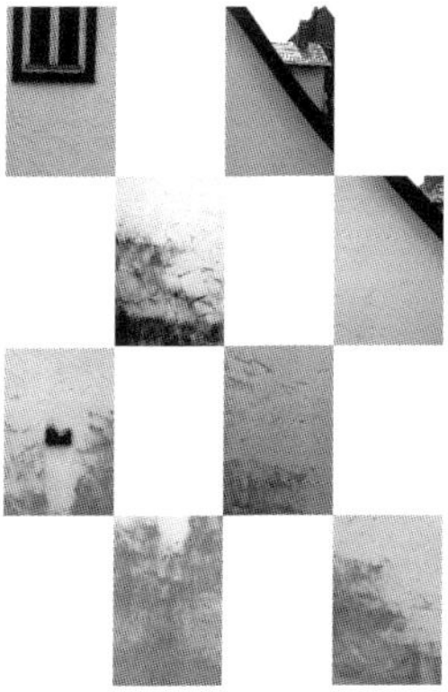

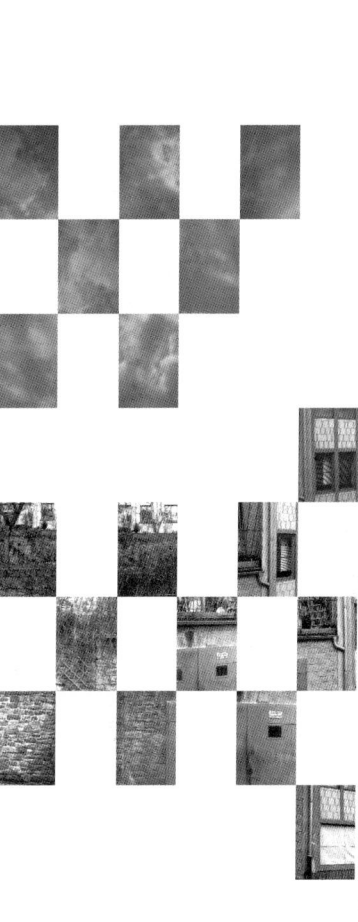

LIVING ROOM

Context?
Ludger Gerdes

The Latin word 'contextus' – from 'contextere', to weave together – means connection of words, coherence. In everyday language, 'context' describes the surroundings in which something is situated, out of which it emerged, and through which it is, to a greater or lesser degree, conditioned. But what do we mean by the context of a house? Is it the houses and streets all around, the neighbourhood with its various eaves heights and pitched roofs, the village church? Do regional building styles make up the context? Is context the history of architecture – since Iktinos, or since Neufert? Is it the people in the surrounding area and how they live that constitute the context of a building? Does context go back to the day the builder first learned the word 'house' from his mother or father? Or is it the history of a particular place, the history of Gelnhausen, or of Hesse… Germany, Europe, the earth, the solar system? Where does context begin; where does it end? When we talk about 'context', do we not also have to talk about political history, legal history, economic history, technological history, behavioural history? And do we not also have to consult sociology, the Office of Statistics, psychoanalysis, studies in ideology, folklore, and so on and so forth? 'Context' means connection – and everything is known to be somehow connected with everything else. We can always expand the context, continuing the multiplication *ad absurdum*.

In short, I believe that the term 'context' is too imprecise, too infinite, to provide a starting-point for discussion, so I will focus instead on a few issues which appear particularly relevant to this project: namely, the way we live, public versus private, the approach to the design.

The Kuhgasse building is a private residence, a living room, an inner sanctum secured by walls. It has a load-bearing structure, incorporating insulation and services, which is entirely covered with a thin cladding of metal. This creates a structure that is invisible from the outside, and a visible exterior which supports nothing but itself. The metal cloaks the structure like a piece of clothing. Not a splendid, elegant dress, but a rather simple one (a light trench coat, perhaps, or a summer suit, a summer dress (with spaghetti straps), a white lab coat, T-shirt or singlet…

Architecture as clothing – the familiar theme is given a new twist through the rhythm of the fenestration on the exterior. The windows are arranged in staggered vertical and horizontal rows, creating an effect more akin to a chessboard than to a conventional house. A new way of playing with the architectural opposition: open versus closed. In the house, opening and closure are equally articulated: neither dominates the appearance of the whole. The outer surface does not refer to traditional tectonics, for here the tectonics are within the cover. What can be seen instead is the repetition of a pattern, or ornament (enjoying a new lease of life, long after being declared dead).

The house will irritate for yet another reason. Conventionally, each floor is marked by a single row of windows: here, the equivalent space contains *two* parallel rows. This has several consequences. It makes the dwarf-house appear larger than it actually is. It allows light to flood in from several directions. And it presents passers-by with a curious display – of an interior with the character of an outdoor garden.

The home is bound up with notions of privacy and intimacy. At home we shed the 'second skin' of our clothing. We also mould the interior according to our tastes, as a 'third skin'. This sometimes makes a visit to other people's homes uncomfortable, holding unwelcome surprises ('If I had known what kind of pictures he had on his walls, many things would have been clearer to me'). The living space is *personal*. It is the place for the things we most enjoy having and doing. At home we are writers and directors, not only of our own actions but also of the dialogues we take part in; even the sets are created by us. Here we can rest, relax, give free rein to our feelings, act out our wishes, desires, neuroses, idiosyncrasies.... Our home represents not only personal safety but also self-realization.

The character of a *private* living room is in a large measure defined by the furnishings and objects it contains. Similarly, the character of the *public* space outside is shaped by the buildings within it. Building is a supremely public matter, because we all spend a portion of our lives in public places, on public streets. We are all affected by buildings, whether we like it or not.

Some people think that a house is successful when it does not attract attention. Like skin and clothing, a house can be inconspicuous, reserved, neutral, indifferent – it can exist without our being conscious of every square inch of its surface. However, it is not possible for everything, everywhere, to be neutral and indifferent; nor is it desirable. A house or a city that has been designed to be plain and reserved is dull and uninspiring. The challenge faced by architects, therefore, is not only to design buildings that are economic, practical, well lit, properly ventilated and ecologically sound, but also to make these buildings act upon people's minds, desires, imagination, memory, creativity and, not least of all, upon their capacity to feel pleasure and displeasure.

'We make our buildings and, accordingly, our buildings make us.' Winston Churchill's quote is justly renowned, as it addresses architecture's crucial social role. But how do we want architecture to affect us? How is this decided? Are there only subjective preferences in democratic pluralism, or are there also generally recognizable means of expression and design?

A building can be given a particular expression through the way in which it engages with a theme or idea. The design can deal with a building's relation to the ground, the way in which it towers, or simply turns a corner. Designs can communicate, too, by expressing a similarity with other forms. From Antiquity to Gehry, there are numerous examples of anthropomorphic or figurative buildings, whereby mass, surface and line are designed in such a way that they can be read as analogies of objects outside of architecture. In this sense, built structures can symbolize a general order, a condition of flexible balance, or some other abstract concept.

There is a further visual creative practice which is particularly pertinent to this project: cohesion. The ancient Greek word *armonia* means connection through meshing and, in this sense, a cohesion or balance of the multiple parts that make up the whole. Disparate objects may co-exist within an expanded network of relationships, without any single object dominating the whole. Such harmony is perhaps the highest achievement that artists of any discipline can accomplish. If an aesthetic design ignores the principle of harmonious cohesion, it may have a short-term sensuous effect, but no lasting intellectual or emotional impact.

Architecture has been described as mother of the visual arts. Traditionally buildings represent not only a relationship to sculpture, painting and ornament, but also the harmony between these different things. In the twentieth century, however, architecture and the visual arts have become separated from each other. Isolated, architecture has certainly become impoverished. At the Kuhgasse house, the architects have encouraged the collaboration of a number of artists. It appears that, in one place at least, the scattered family members will be reunited. This will be interesting – perhaps even harmonious.

This is a condensed version of the German original.

Covered by Sky, Open to Ground
Martha LaGess

I   When Robert Venturi published *Complexity and Contradiction* in 1966, he initiated a dramatic reaction against the perceived tedium of contemporary architectural practice. More than thirty years later, the architectural scene still benefits from Postmodernism's 'adjustments' to Modernism; mainstream practice today is far more varied than it was in the mid 1960s. Nevertheless, there is a pattern visible in current work. On the one hand, there are commercial firms who have continued all this time as if nothing has happened; apart from the presence of superficial stylistic flourishes, there is no evidence that the architectural or philosophical arguments of Postmodernism have affected them. On the other hand, among the less innocent, there are three definite groups: those pursuing an interest in history, including a technological future-history, those using the authority (and power) of 'scientific' methods, especially computer processes intended to limit design's 'subjectivity', and those such as Seifert and Stöckmann, who are searching art practice to find a potentially fruitful source of 'technology' transfer.

II   The Living Room project tries to behave like an artwork. It is an extraordinary house with an ordinary shape, which encourages us to think of houses differently. According to the architects' own project description, 'The house is designed with five artists and a poet, and is intended to become a platform for various artistic positions. It is hoped that these disparate positions will together form a new context with which to address the public. It will wait for a response.' But why would architects want to make their own house an artists' platform? Or to put the point more forcefully, why would architects want to tear down a seventeenth-century structure and build a house strongly conditioned by modern art on the same site? Is architecture now so removed from the arts that artists can be invited into an architect's home as strangers?

Before the seventeenth century, architecture was definitely one of the arts. This connection took place through the craft of building itself, and also through architectural drawings. But today there is inevitably a gap between the artwork which is most architectural and the work of architecture which is most artistic. No matter how many similarities we find between them, it is unlikely that the two disciplines can be reunited. This is not only because so many of the architectural crafts have evolved into industrial products and engineering since the seventeenth century; arguably, architecture is no longer an art primarily because the content and social position of the arts themselves have changed. When scientific and industrial procedures and processes decreased the social value of the craftsperson's skill, the arts became increasingly preoccupied with the artist's 'subjectivity'.

By the eighteenth century the gradual development of the sciences had led to their divorce from the newly secularized 'humanities'. Architecture was left with a dilemma: it didn't really know which side to join. Design, especially through its association with drawing, links architecture with the arts (and humanities). Like an artwork, a work of architecture seems personal to its author and dependent on unscientific design techniques. At the same time, construction links architecture with engineering (and the 'natural' sciences). As an engineered object, architecture is something which deals with impersonal forces, and behaves, we think, in accordance with a complex interaction of universal laws. But neither affiliation seems to characterize architecture fully. Architecture seems neither as personal as an art object nor as impersonal as a work of engineering. Instead, the role of architecture is to be occupied, to synthesize a relationship between person and world. Its occupation need not be actual; it is enough if the project was intended to be, could be, or is symbolically *occupied* (especially by the gods – or God). The use of a building is much less important than the intention for human beings to be present within it. The house is the simplest case: all other building types are house derivatives.

III While at university, the architects of the Living Room project perceived a difference between the ideas and methods of art students they met, and those of their own department. This, they say, motivated them to include artists on their architectural team. (These are not craftspeople either, but unabashed 'fine' artists.) The artworks set the Living Room apart from other houses, because for a long time it has been almost unthinkable to have an extensive art programme as an integral part of an architect's house design (with the exception of artworks by the architects themselves, and regardless of the artistic pretentions of Postmodernism following Venturi). Certainly by the time Loos wrote 'Ornament and Crime', architecture and the arts had already parted ways.

In the Living Room, the house makes way for the artworks. The architectural shell is a neutral boundary, a division line with no thickness. This could make the outside pure exterior landscape and the inside pure interior room, but the ground itself violates this division. When we visit an abandoned building in a state of ruin, we often find that its roof is damaged or missing though the walls remain. If we don't look up, conditions seem ordinary; but when we do, the clear separation between outside and inside evaporates. To see open sky in the place of a ceiling can give a sense of freedom, but at the same time we can also experience sadness for the building's fragility, so like our own.

The outside world breaks into the Living Room, but here there is a motif familiar from Tarkovsky's films: the infiltration takes place from underneath; the roof is sound enough, but not the floor. This building is covered by sky and 'open' to ground, an arrangement which shows that its architects thumb their noses at architectural positivism – the tendency of architects to legitimize their designs through the use of semi-scientific and/or industrial procedures – and resist the Cartesian anti-sensualism which supports the notion of an opposition between 'the subjective' (which is personal and sensory) and 'the objective' (which is impersonal, abstract and immaterial).

In his *Meditations* Descartes argues that apparently concrete sensory objects are not necessarily concrete at all, but potentially ephemeral, unreliable illusions. He recommends mathematical concepts as a means of avoiding the deception of the senses, reasoning that mathematics is an entirely mental phenomenon, therefore not subject to deceptive variation. Our culture still follows his argument; our individual, sensual understanding of what seems to be 'actual' soil is at war with the generally accepted notion that there is a 'real' world which is not a matter of personal experience, but of an objective order perceptible only through science.

IV I suppose this project would seem quite different if we didn't know about the seventeenth-century house. After all, it has been standing there on its site in Gelnhausen ever since Descartes was alive. Whatever the success of the new house, we mourn the old one, even though we know its structure was rotten. Despite youth and freshness, a new building is no substitute for an ancient one that has seen so much.

But imagine coming upon the new house long after the construction is complete, after the publicity is over, after the old house has been forgotten. What would we think if we could put aside everything – the texts, photographs, plans, exhibition – that preceded the house itself? Would we imagine that this was only a house? Or won't the artworks hidden inside demand their public? As everyone knows, a house famous for its architecture generates some conflict of interest between the people who live there and the architects' (and artists') audience. The residents expect privacy, but those who have seen the house published will always approach the Living Room as if it were their own.

Painting
Ludger Gerdes

For the Kuhgasse house I have drawn some simple motifs, images of expanses of water, of bodies built and otherwise. These motifs (and/or others like them) can be printed or painted onto the wall spaces between the windows of the building. I think of them as adornment. They are intended to stimulate pleasure as well as the conception of thoughts and ideas.

Buildings carry loads. My works carry meaning. Buildings can bear a variety of loads, my works can prompt a variety of interpretations.

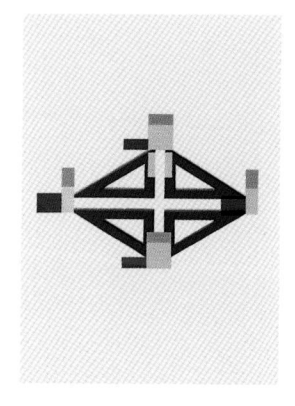

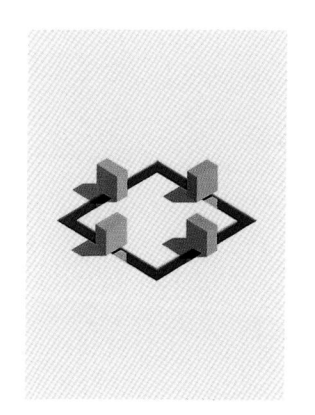

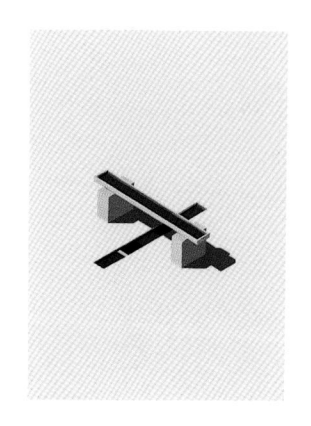

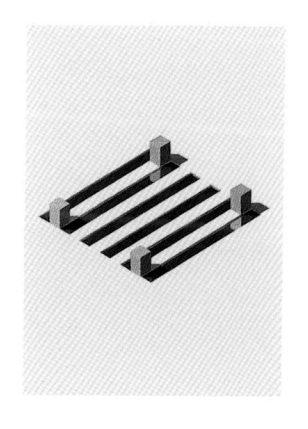

LIVING ROOM

Light: Flicker
Charly Steiger

'Flicker' is a computer-operated light installation developed in response to the architecture and specific context of the new building designed by Seifert and Stöckmann. Boxes fitted with electronic flashes (two apiece) are set at regular intervals into the facade/load-bearing structure. Glass-covered viewing slits allow people outside to look into the boxes and see 'extracts' of the former 'interior' modelled after Spellman and Murff's 'Here and Gone' mapping of the old house. The surfaces inside the boxes are covered with a pigment which emits a fluorescent glow when charged by a timed electronic flash. Then the glow fades, and the forms inside slowly recede into darkness. From the street three stages of this process can be perceived:

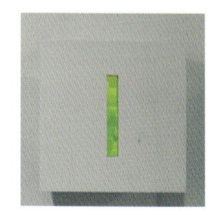

- dark slits with no flash, no glow and hardly any optical information
- shimmering green slits with afterglow, spatial perception
- flickering white slits with flash cycle, a view of the interior and changing spatial perception.

'Flicker' makes reference to specific elements of the architecture: the strength of the walls (the dimensions of the installations), the regularity of the fenestration (the positioning of the viewing slits), the planar surfaces, the use/avoidance of the public space adjoining the house, and the obvious slope of the site (which causes different viewing heights). In terms of content, the work explicitly refers to the use of the house's surroundings as a passage. Passers-by come upon a situation that can be handled in a variety of ways: on the one hand, the brightly flickering flashes and green afterglow demand their attention; on the other hand, giving in to this 'attraction' requires a show of attention which runs counter to 'casual' modes of observation. In order to gain more information the viewer has to adopt the pose of a voyeur. The rapid succession of flashes will trigger a variety of associations, probably not all of them pleasant. It is impossible to predict what course each individual will choose: approach or flight, submission or aggression.

A second important point of reference is the conspicuous provision of windows that, through their quantity and position, provide exaggerated opportunities for looking into the house. Flicker continues the theme of the house's perforated outer skin, but in a qualitatively different manner: if passers-by dare to look through a viewing slit, what they see is not the inside of the house, but rather the inside of a kind of chamber whose installations will require personal decoding.

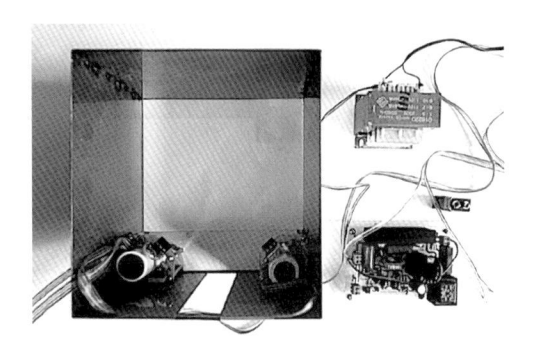

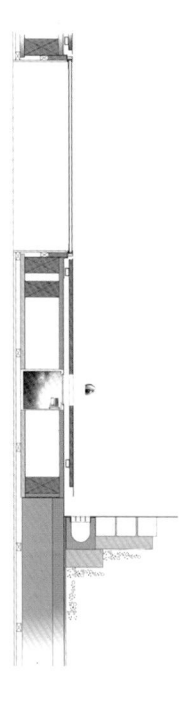

Noise: Transformation
Achim Wollscheid

The right, front and left walls of the Kuhgasse house each contain an integrated transformation system which consists of two microphones, a sound-computer and two loudspeakers. Environmental noise is recorded, transformed via programmed composition-presets, and emitted in real time. A control unit in the house enables the degree and direction of the transformation to be adjusted: from soft to strong, from inside to outside, or from outside to inside.

LIVING ROOM   43

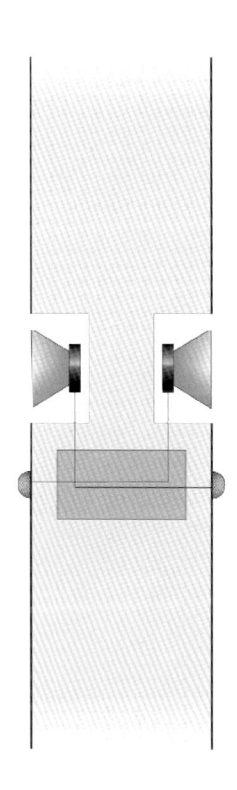

```
noise noise noise noise nois
ise noise noise  ise noise noise
e noise noise      noise noise no
noise noise        ise noise nois
 e noise noi       ise noise n
 oise noise        oise noise
 ise noise         se noise
 noise no          oise nois
 ise noise         se noise
 e noise      sound   noise n
 noise no          oise nois
 se noise          noise n
 oise nois         ise noise
 noise no          oise nois
```

```
                 s
               se n
              se noise
             noise nois
            ise noise noi
            ise noise noise
            noise noise noi
            ise noise noise
  sound     se noise noise n     sound
            noise noise noi
            se noise noise r
            oise noise noisi
            se noise noise n
```

Transformation mode a – transformation directed from the inside towards the outside.
Transformation mode b – transformation directed from the outside towards the inside.

ACHIM WOLLSCHEID

Context!
(An Alternative View)
Achim Wollscheid

Programme. In the house on Kuhgasse, a concept of habitation is developed into a staged experience. The building programme creates a living room that is, dually, a room for living in and a room that lives. The scene is set by everyday objects that are combined in new ways: the outdoor garden here becomes an indoor space; the windows form a grid-like pattern; the bedroom is a cell detached from the building envelope. Yet this montage of displaced objects is not the whole story of the work. There is also a specific idea of function, coherence, correctness; an idea of how both objects and behaviour should be organized within a house. The contradiction between these two approaches is mediated. 'Oppositional staging' overlaps with 'pragmatic incorporation' in a manner comparable with the operation of 'presets' in computer-generated music. Presets are in principle interchangeable. Each has a programmed 'sound' which, however abstract, fulfils a pragmatic function through its integration into the whole of the piece. Even if the single preset is complex, questionable, autonomous or volatile, as a segment of a sequence it contributes to the creation of something useful, perhaps even habitual.

In contrast to this internal differentiation, the shell of the house, though traditional in shape, presents itself as a visible reduction – as a neutral, almost off-putting exterior with a grid-like, interrupted opacity. The puncturing of the facade gives views inside, opening up the opportunity for a partial decoding of the building's purpose, yet the overall effect is one of object-like self-containment. To extend the sound analogy, one might view the neighbouring buildings as the 'piece' of music into which the house, as a transformed preset, is inserted. The house integrates itself by concealing its internal complexity, but in so doing it exposes the preset, heterogeneous character of its surroundings.

Conglomerate. The Kuhgasse house not only reacts to but actively participates in a contemporary phenomenon – the conglomerate. The conglomerate displays no logic in its formation, but consists of variously defined juxtapositions and successions in which the placement of the objects – their proximity to each other – has no bearing on the meaning. The conglomerate is, prototypically, a heap that can be augmented or eroded, its different segments shifting at different times. The conglomerate has no centre; it is, in the literal sense of the term, confused. The conglomerate has, of course, an underlying order, but does not express it: the rules that guide its composition are too numerous, relating not to the conglomerate alone but to all the things and processes that may have an impact upon it. To give an example: ongoing social conditions may largely be regarded as conglomerates dispersed over time. The existence and form of a social grouping (e.g. the inhabitants of an urban industrial area) can only be explained by reference to a multitude of external factors. A snapshot of such a condition has no explanatory value: it is nothing more than a detail, grasping an individual element. Correspondingly, a built house – as a consequence and expression of this condition – is an 'unintentional' detail: to live is to be present in a detail.

As I see it, this detail condition is assimilated within the staged reduction of space in the Kuhgasse house – for example, in the minimum 'sleeping cell', or the bathroom and kitchen stowed in a 'multi-functional wall' (a quotation from aircraft design). As the detail has no intrinsic motivation, no content beyond the fact of its being a detail, practical considerations become the basis for an aesthetic strategy.

Implant. Within the silhouette of the old Lemon House arises a new structure defined by new materials and new parameters. An implant replaces the entire body. If the new house provokes an element of mirth, it may be because this substitution also identifies the life in the surrounding bodies – that is, the houses in the so-called historic district of Gelnhausen – as a kind of implant, where the past remains unexperienced.

Provocation and Experiment. The Living Room upsets the normal 'structures' of practical and discursive orders, to see how people will react. The context of the house, the old town, broadly resists discussion. There is scarely any debate about 'innovative building' (aside from the written histories, which in any case emphasize the unusual over the commonplace). Innovation usually means a new way of conservation (and in this respect, Gelnhausen is like any other town). 'New' architecture tends to be sanctioned only for public buildings. If it happens at all, it is broached not in terms of intervention, but in terms of careful addition.

The Kuhgasse house breaks this mould. It intervenes, insinuates itself, by taking on another's skin. It is like a surprise-guest who, far from being shy, touches people, assuming a commanding presence. The discussion, which would normally be limited to familiar themes, is somehow inverted. The house upsets conventionally 'structured' orders. Its transformation can be seen as a challenge – an experiment aimed at provoking a reaction from the people and the environment around it.

Play. Some houses have play areas. Usually these are intermediate zones which see only occasional use: a garden, balcony or patio. In contrast to the rest of the living space, such areas are a platform for public statements of an aesthetic nature. (Though it is uncertain whether the aesthetics serve to conceal the purpose of the actions that take place, or whether the purpose of the actions themselves is to aestheticize.) Affixed to houses like placards, these spaces are read as a vital element, as legible text, as information. This convention works provided that such displays are clearly differentiated from and subordinate to the rest of the building, and a strict hierarchy is observed: support (floor, background, etc.), objects (trees, chairs, tables, etc.), information (moving person).

However, a problem arises if, as in the case of the Kuhgasse house, the 'play areas' compete with the strictly utilitarian spaces, or are even congruent with them. The confusion about what is being played where, and by whom, blurs the boundary that normally separates the symbolic from the real. Prior to demolition, the Lemon House is to be covered with a net of carnations: both the net and the house will become simultaneously signifier and signified. Similarly, the new house can be seen both as a net of stereotypical square openings contained in a frame (the wall), and as a wall displaying an unusual pattern. For practically every object and situation in the house, the relation between the support and the thing supported, between background and foreground, is virtually interchangeable. The house as anagram.

This idea of interchangeability could conceivably be extended to the relations of the various unconnected 'object-signifiers'. The house could be imagined as a three-dimensional distributor, with each object, each surface, functioning simultaneously as support and thing supported, as signifier or as background to a constantly redefined number of other signifiers. This cross-referencing overturns set assumptions and forces us to invent and practise new strategies.

Book. The Living Room also contains artworks in a variety of media, made by artists who have been involved in the development of the project from the outset. The intersection of architectural programme, space and displacement is thus augmented by the intersection of the artists' spatial concepts and installations. In a similar manner, a conglomerate of texts develops in this book. The texts oscillate between internal and external themes. Some address solely the house; others refer to the context, or to a specific artwork. This book, their *raison d'être*, functions, like the house, as a distributor. Depending on perspective, one could read the texts and images as paraphrases of a possible internal cohesion, as a programme, or, conversely, as a montage which links the book to the conglomerate outside.

This text is a condensed version of the German original.

Sculpture

Wolfgang Luy

Designs for tables, handrails, etc.

real table real real table real real real
real real x=y real real nature real real
real real real real dialogue real real real
circle real real leave real real real real
real real real real real real real leave real real
real leave real dialogue real real real x=y real real
real house real real real real house real real

LIVING ROOM

A Heart's Project
Peter Cook

It is a rare thing to put one's heart into a project. Everything in present culture forces one into a position of irrational and immeasurable particularity that unleashes the cry of 'wilful' (from those who most likely don't have enough spirit or invention to find their heart, anyway). To return to one's roots is another fraught territory. Generally speaking, the feeble and the frightened or those seeking accolades for being the big fish in a small pond are the ones who go back to the point of departure. To reintegrate the old typology is another tiresome habit, very fashionable these days. Discovering that the old form and the old ways that contributed to it have a knitted-together logic is very comforting – and conducive to dismissing all invention and experimentation as threatening. To suggest that art has its place either in the gallery (where the curatorship of the space and the philosophizing of the catalogue act as a safety net) or in the street (where populism can act as a useful territory for the blurring of intentional edges) is highly convenient. To create a total place for a special confrontation of artists, on the other hand, is dangerous stuff, which calls for knowledge of and sensitivity towards those artists.

In all these four conditions, Gabi Seifert and Götz Stöckmann have acted heroically and, I believe, honestly. Their hearts are here with this project. A long-developed understanding of the pros and cons of familiarity – with both place and people – bolsters them against any loss of nerve. Gelnhausen has its own local culture, and Seifert and Stöckmann have their own distinct conception of the place – memories tied to childhood and family and the temptation of nearby Frankfurt city, with both its inhospitable side and its airborne window to the world. They are now quite simply *old* enough to deal again with their home town.

To take the shape of the old 'cottage' typology and then 'gut' it, keeping the window type but repeating it – as if it were just a piece of an ongoing mathematical graphic – ironically leaves something creatively open, almost a *tabula rasa* condition!

It is to be hoped that the various artists who have been invited to participate will have the same sense of occasion: that they will consider the envelope and the irony of the setting with the same degree of wit as their fellow artists – the architects.

The project is meticulously thought through, and will undoubtedly establish Seifert and Stöckmann in their rightful position as key architects of their generation, quite able to talk back to the Mathildenhöhe in Darmstadt, to Cranbrook in Detroit, or to the Secession building in Vienna, where a similar heart is displayed through a form of seance between architects and artists.

Farewell to the old house: Bye Bye Kuhgasse 15.

LIVING ROOM

Das Haus ist der Mundraum

Thomas Kling

                                              das haus ist der mundraum.
                                    das haus ist text seiner bewohner.

                           ist es erlaubt, vom atem, vom durchatmen
                               der bewohner in einem haus zu sprechen?

                            ist es erlaubt, vom atem der generationen
                            zu sprechen, die in dem haus gewohnt haben?

                 schlechter atem im ungelüfteten haus. gerüche
im treppenhaus und aus den fenstern der nachbarschaft.

                        atem, der aus dem mund der wöchnerin geht.
                           schneller atem, rasselnd, eines sterbenden.

                die fenster sind geöffnet. die tür zur straße geht auf,
eine person verläßt das haus. sie zögert, dreht sich um

                    betritt das haus abermals, kehrt wieder mit einem
                  gegenstand, den sie vergessen hat. es ist 10 uhr 35.

                ist es erlaubt, vom atem der hausbewohner und ihrer
                vergeßlichkeit zu sprechen? von der geschwindigkeit

                in der ein verlassenes haus ein verlassenes haus wird?
                ist es erlaubt, zu sagen, daß die steine unvermutet ins

haus gelangen? ist es erlaubt, zu sagen, daß hier große
steine mitten in den wohnraum gelangt sind, dorthin,

wo sie nicht hingehören? was werden, sohn, die nachbarn
sagen? junge, hast du denn darüber nachgedacht, was die

nachbarn sagen werden? die nachbarn atmen in ihren häusern,
mutter, sie verlassen ihr haus, kehren um, weil sie etwas

vergessen haben. aber junge, was werden deine nachbarn
sagen, wenn sie erfahren, daß der garten im haus ist?

mutter, mein garten atmet im haus, atmet wie meine
nachbarn atmen. jeder hat pflanzen im haus, mutter!

ich kehre um, ich drehe das haus um, weil ich etwas
vergessen habe. ich habe das haus auf den kopf gestellt!

ist es erlaubt, junge, davon zu sprechen, daß das haus
so sehr atmet, daß der erste stock auf die strasse fahren kann!

mutter, alle nachbarn werden mitfahren wollen, wenn sie sehen,
was mein haus alles kann. das haus gähnt, es atmet mutter!

das haus erlebt seine bewohner, es öffnet den mundraum.
das haus atmet, es ist der text seiner bewohner.

das haus ist zuhause bei sich, es zeigt sich. es zeigt
die summe seines atems: das haus ist der mundraum.

Biographical Notes

M Christine Boyer is the William R Kenan, jr. Professor at the School of Architecture, Princeton University. She has written extensively about American and European urbanism. Her most recent publication is *CyberCities* (Princeton Architectural Press, 1996).

Peter Cook has his own practice, with Christine Hawley, and is Professor of Architecture at the Bartlett School of Architecture, University College, London.

Ludger Gerdes was born in 1954 in Lower Saxony. He studied art with Lothar Baumgarten and Timm Ulrichs in Münster, and with Gerhard Richter in Düsseldorf. He has created numerous permanent installations for public spaces.

David Heymann is Associate Dean for Undergraduate Programs in the School of Architecture at the University of Texas at Austin, and has his own architectural practice with Michael Underhill and Laura Miller.

Ottmar Hörl studied art in Frankfurt am Main and Düsseldorf, and in 1985 co-founded the experimental group Formalhaut, with Gabriela Seifert and Götz Stöckmann. He has won several prizes independently and with Formalhaut.

Thomas Kling is a poet, essayist and publisher. He was awarded the 1997 Peter Huchel Prize for his volume of poetry, *morsch* (Suhrkamp, 1996).

Martha LaGess teaches at the Architectural Association, London, and practises with Michael McNamara as LaMa Architects.

Wolfgang Luy studied art at the Kunstakademie, Düsseldorf, and has taught at the Hochschule für Gestaltung, Offenbach. His work has been exhibited throughout Europe and in the USA.

Scott Murff has been working in the partnership Biegner–Murff in Arizona since 1995 and has completed several residential and office buildings. He studied architecture at the Cooper Union, New York and has taught at Arizona State University.

Gabriela Seifert studied architecture at Frankfurt Polytechnic and the Staedelschule, where she was the Meisterschüler of Peter Cook in 1985. Co-founded the architectural practice Seifert + Stöckmann in 1984, and the experimental group Formalhaut in 1985. Chairs the Institut für Raumgestaltung at the University of Innsbruck.

Catherine Spellman is Assistant Professor of Architecture at Arizona State University. She has taught and worked in the USA and Europe, and is now in independent practice.

Götz Stöckmann studied architecture at Frankfurt Polytechnic, the Staedelschule, and the AA, where he won the Diploma School Prize in 1983. He worked for Haus–Rucker–Co before setting up the architectural practice Seifert + Stöckmann in 1984, and the experimental group Formalhaut in 1985. He teaches at the Architectural Association in London.

Charly Steiger lives and works in Frankfurt am Main. She has created site-specific installations using various media (video, light) and music projects in Germany, Spain, Belgium, the Netherlands, France, Hungary, Poland, Austria and Australia.

Dalibor Vesely was born in Prague and studied architecture and art history. He is currently teaching in Cambridge, working as a consultant, and writing on the politics of architecture.

Achim Wollscheid is an artist, writer and teacher who creates both recorded and installation work, collaborating with a number of artists and musicians. He is a member of Selektion, an organization for the production and distribution of information systems.

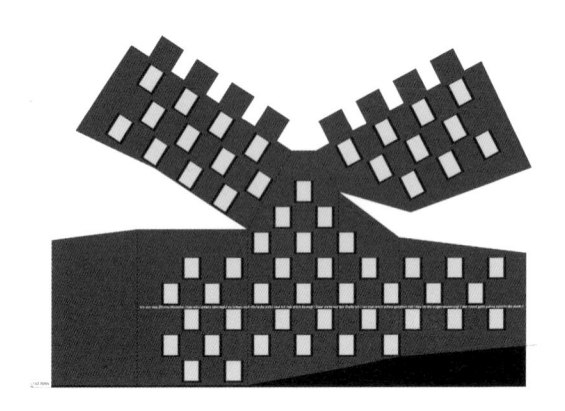

The new house will initially be covered by asphalt sheeting inscribed with an epigram by Thomas Kling.

ich war das Zitrone-Häusche/
hab mirs anders überlegt/
es haben hier die leute sich/
und ich hab mich bewegt//
zwar stehe auf der stelle ich/
wo man mich schon gesehen hat/
das ist die augn-änderung!/
der mund geht auf – es spricht die stadt//